Play Your Game

Play Your Game

Marriage wins!

Shelly Rudo Chapinduka

Play Your Game. Marriage Wins!

Email: shelly_chapinduka@yahoo.com

DEDICATION

I dedicate this book to my dad; father God, my Lord and Savior Jesus Christ and the Holy Ghost. They are the best mentors one could ever have. I would strongly recommend them to you. They have given me strength to enjoy my marriage in good times and in bad times.

God the father, Jesus our Lord and Savior and the Holy Ghost are excellent in showing you the best way to live a married life.

ACKNOWLEDGEMENT

I want to thank my husband Paul Chapinduka for sharing his life with me in matrimony. It is almost 37 years we have been together. I am still looking forward to having many more years of fun, cuddling, laughter and loving each other.

I would be one of many to say, "It is not the number of years one has been married that matters the most, but it is the numberless times the husband and wife are willing to forgive each other, and start all over again."

I want to thank our children who have always had a positive attitude towards whatever we are doing, or want to do. Parents should never underestimate the help they can get from their children. They are techno savvy and can be of great help.

I want to thank my late parents Emily and Salathiel Matemera, who are cheering and watching me run my race until I finish my course.

I want to thank my grandparents Marita and Phiri, who deposited in me a desire and an appreciation for marriage. I think I was only eleven or so years when I visited them at the farm. They worked on a corn farm and lived in a one-room mud house. Their condition did not take away the love they had for each other. They learnt how to enjoy the moment with the little they had. They respected each other so much and were always together.

I remember promising myself at such a tender age, that when I get married; my marriage was going to be like my grandparents. I admired the way they were friends. They loved and communicated with each other with faces that glowed with admiration, and adoration.

Almost every day, my grandparents made sure that their day ended with laughter and jovial-hand clapping. I am glad that they deposited in me an ever-increasing love for marriage. I truly miss them.

I want to thank all my friends who have encouraged me to write this book. I would not have had this boldness to write this book had it not been for some of you.

Thank you very much.

CONTENTS

INTRODUCTION

What we are constantly thinking about eventually becomes our passion. My passion is to see marriages that were once on the verge of a breaking point, come back together and start afresh. Marriage works when both parties are willing to work at it.

Marriage is not a hundred meter dash but a marathon. It gains momentum when we observe and pay attention to all the road signs of our marriages. Passing red lights and not paying attention to all cross roads of our marriages will cost us our relationships. It takes wisdom, knowledge, and understanding to build a long-term marriage.

It is priceless to see a husband and a wife who once hated each other with a passion, forgives, hugs and love each other again. My question then to you is, "Are you doing all it takes to make your marriage work?" If not, please try your level best to make things right. It takes love, perseverance, and forgiveness for marriage to work. **We do not keep grudges**, we forget those things that are behind and we keep focusing on what is ahead.

The teachings in this book focus mainly on helping married couples and those who are thinking of getting married. We are going to learn on how to separate the past and the present issues from contaminating our day-to-day life. Holding on to the past and constantly reminding each other of past failures does not resolve the present issues in our marriages. Issues are to be dealt with as they come, and couples have to learn to live in the now than in yesterday's problems.

Gone are the days of sweeping our marriage problems under the rug. It is time we deal with the problems head on. We have to fight for our marriages and our children. We do not take the fight lying down; we rise up, dust ourselves, and keep fighting until we win.

"Choose you this day whom you will serve; ... but as for me and my house we will serve the Lord."

Joshua 24:15.

Marriage wins! Marriage is the greatest life style that can ever happen between two people who love each other. We play the game of marriage until we win. It is a mind and heart game. As a man thinks so is he. We should not quench the desire of getting married no matter what could have happened before or after marriage.

There is always room to start all over again. We do not get married to see if it works. We get married because we love each other. We look forward to spending the rest of our lives together in harmony; loving each other until death do us part.

Marriage is a journey. It is a covenant, a commitment and it works best as a team. I liken it to driving a car. We do not stop at speed bumps; we slow down, go over them and keep on driving until we get to our destination.

The more we look in the rear view mirror (always reminding each other of past failures) the longer it will take us to get to our destination.

We grow in our marriages by taming our tongue and being patient with each other.

"Death and life are in the power of the tongue: and they that love it shall eat the fruit thereof."

Proverbs 18:21.

Our marriages should leave behind footprints of legacy, the legacy of love and perseverance. It gets better with time it is like a diamond in the rough. The greater the heat, the shinier it becomes. **So let your marriage shine!**

Chapter 1

GAME DAY
IS FINALLY HERE!

The day almost everyone was waiting for had come! The day the Dallas Cowboys were going to play the Green Bay Packers!

The game was at the Dallas Cowboys home. The sun was shining, a cool breeze was blowing and there was no rain in sight. It was just a beautiful day!

The sidewalks were jammed with people walking to the stadium. Fans, family and friends were coming out in droves to the Arlington AT&T STADIUM. We could hear loud music, noise and shouting from afar and the excitement was so high and contagious. Game day was finally here!

The grounds were mesmerized with the smell of barbequing and tailgating was all over the place. Fans were ready for the game, and both teams were ready to play their game. The young and the old were proudly wearing their favorite t/shirts with names and numbers of their favorite players engraved on them. The grand stands looked so beautiful with blue and white shirts for the Cowboys, green and yellow shirts for the Green Bay Packers. It was game time!

The Dallas Cowboys had played very well during the season and were now focusing on the Super Bowl. They were only two games away in order to qualify for the Super Bowl. Our mindsets were that the Dallas Cowboys were going to win. They were not going to lose at home, no, not at all. Those who remember this day, your stomach should be starting to knot up again. It was so stressful and tense watching this game. The game started and both sides of the teams started cheering.

The Cowboys started slow and were behind with quite a huge margin. It was not much of a surprise because that is how they have been playing the whole season; they would always come back, so it was not a big deal for them to start slow.

Twice the Dallas Cowboys caught up from behind, and the momentum was increasing on their side. They would call time out, gather, call the play, advice, and go back to play.

I was home glued to the television praying and begging God that the Cowboys would win. I would watch the game for a little bit, run to my bedroom kneel down and literally beg God for the Cowboys to win. It is amazing what goes on in the homes during game season. There is shouting, loud noises, jumping up and down just as much as it is at the grand stands.

The game was promising, and the Dallas Cowboys had winning written all over their faces. We were going to win no two ways about it...that is what I was thinking.

Time was ticking, only a few seconds left to close the deal. It was within those few seconds left that the Green Bay Packers quarterback threw the ball to his teammate and that catch changed the whole ball game!

All of a sudden, the grand stands went quiet; it was as if one could hear the pin drop. The unpredictable was about to happen. Time had run out for the Dallas Cowboys to come back and they lost to the Green Bay Packers 34, Dallas Cowboys 31. It was unbelievable! Oh, my God... it still feels like yesterday.

Usually when a team loses, people start blaming and name-calling, not this time; Dallas Cowboys played to the very end. Infect both teams gave all they got!

Even though the Dallas Cowboys and their fans left the grounds sad, we could see a promising team, a team that was going to win the following year. They truly played their game!

One might ask, "So what has this story to do with marriage?" This story has all the elements needed in order for marriage to work.

These elements are practice, hustle and touchdown. It does not matter how many times the marriage has been knocked down; get up, **Play Your Game** until you win your Super bowl!

4

Chapter 2

PRACTICE,

HUSTLE & TOUCHDOWN

Practice

P ractice makes perfect. Sometimes we feel like practicing and sometimes we do not. If we are to play the game to win, we have to be prepared to practice in season and off-season. Whether snowing, raining or cold, the competition still goes on. It takes a lot of discipline and a lot of practice in order to be fit for the game.

The team has to be in one accord, and in tune with its head and sideline coaches. It has to be teachable; otherwise, it will give the coaches a hard time to train and communicate with them.

The same principles apply to marriage. The husband and wife have to be mentally prepared to practice, hustle and play in stressful environments. They should be prepared to practice and play against all odds. Marriage can be stressful sometimes; therefore, the couple has to know when to call time out, and when to continue playing. Both parties have to understand fully the language, rules and regulations of their game.

Every day in practice, we are flexing our marriage muscles. We are learning how to tame our tongue. We practice on how to talk to each other with respect and honor.

A successful marriage has to have God the Father as the head coach, Jesus our Lord and Savior and the Holy Spirit as the sideline coaches. They are not focusing on your failures as such, but they want your commitment.

Husband and wife have to keep on building on the basics that they know. They have to learn from those who are making it and continue practicing on what they have learnt.

Occasionally our minds play tricks on us by controlling and dominating us. They tell us that it is not practice day today therefore; we should just go ahead and relax.

If we are not careful, we can miss the whole week of practice listening to our minds. By the time the game is around, we will have gone rusty and cannot win the game.

Daily we have to stop the negativity and tell our minds to be sober and vigilant. Procrastination in marriage will cost us if we are not paying attention.

Ignoring issues that need our attention makes us rusty and unable to move forward. We just do not do things randomly, or rather impulsively; we have to think before we act. We have to train our minds to think about winning all the time.

Practice forces us to be committed. Even when there is no game to play, practice and every day, communication should continue in order to keep the team on one accord.

Hustle

Marriage is not a fly by night, nor a hit and run. It is not a game for neither the lazy nor the immature, but for the mature and strong in heart and mind. It is a survival for the fittest.

Hustling is stopping the opponent from getting the ball. The players are aware of who play what and when they are a team. Hustling is giving your all in order to get the intended results.

There is a lot of hustling in the football match. The teams fight to keep the ball in their courts. Big men pull each other down just to defend and keep the ball within their team. They play with all their strength and might. Their focus is to stop the opponent from getting the ball.

The same attitude is required among married couples. Remember it is teamwork, not playing against each other, but for each other. The couple's mindset is to stop the opponent from getting the ball. Couples have to give all they got when it comes to standing and keeping what is theirs.

The husband and wife have to make sure that they do not loose respect and honor for each other no matter how tense the situations might be.

Hustling helps the couples to decipher what works and does not work. Most couples get married without counting the cost. It takes time and patience to build a long lasting marriage. The couples that are willing to hustle will soon enjoy the benefits of their marriage if they do not give up.

Hustling makes the marriage a bed of beautiful roses. Sometimes we bleed trying to get to the blooming rose but that does not stop us from getting to the rose. It is through hustling that we are able to cut off the thorny stems of our marriage in order to smell the roses.

Planning and doing things together can be a challenge. There has to be a quick identification of those things that so easily beset us. Hustling allows couples to disagree and yet learn how to get back together in agreement.

The greatest asset in hustling is a bond of true friendship, freedom of love and expression. Couples who invest in their marriage by giving each other the freedom of choice reap greater dividends.

Marriage gets difficult when couples do not know how to be friends. Friendship means you are more aware of what makes the other happy and not so happy. You rule your tongue and you are easy to love. There has to be freedom of expression without the fear of rejection.

There has to be a willingness of spending time together. Spending time together makes the couples see each other's weaknesses and strengths, which even makes the relationship stronger, lovable and peaceful.

Hustling is not my way or no way, it is our way as a team. There is a lot of pushing and pulling down. The team is in one accord and the goal is a touchdown. The team players hustle to keep the ball because their focus is to get the ball to the end zone.

It takes passion to do what we love. Marriage is lovable when the team knows how to hustle. The aim of hustling is to make sure that the opponent does not get the ball. It is teamwork, the husband and wife routing for the same goal. When you love your spouse, you hustle for them no matter how challenging it might be. Husband and wife should hustle for their marriage. Wise communication and love should be their greatest anchor.

Touchdown

In order to have a touchdown, there should not be a mix-up on roles. Both parties have a different part to play in their game of marriage. The quarterback in reference to marriage is the husband, and the wife is the wide receiver. The quarterback needs a lot of encouragement when playing this game.

Trust and honor is the main anchor. He has to know when to pass the ball before the other team gets to him and he loses the ball. The receiver should be fast enough, a sprinter, always in a position to catch the ball. Her focus is to take the ball to the end zone. A lot of pressure is on the quarterback (husband) from his team and opponent team.

He has to be healthy and ready to play for long hours than the rest of the team. He is the most studied and gone after the hardest by the opposite team. They want to tackle him before he even throws the ball.

The wife (wide receiver) has to be trusted, that she can run with the vision and make a touchdown.

She is in constant practice for her sprinting, and makes sure that her hands are strong enough to catch the ball and keep it.

The question then becomes, "Wife, are you prepared to take this position?"

This position is not for the weak, but for the strong. It requires more alertness and no room for absent-mindedness. When we realize how critical our positions are in marriage then we will not take the game of marriage for granted, we will play our game to the end.

Whether we win or lose, we should not forget our fans or our cheerleaders. We should thank them because they are our momentum. Make friends with those that respect your marriage, those are your fans and cheerleaders. They come handy when things get tough.

Chapter 3

WHY IS COMMUNICATION IMPORTANT?

C ommunication is a way of conveying a message between two people, groups or communities. It is the desire of the one sending the message to know that the receiver has understood the message. Their communication antenna has to have its signal in place in order to transmit the right messages. Husband and wife should have their communication skills intact so that they are able to receive the messages they are signaling to each other.

Whether good or bad signal, there is always a response to every type of communication. This is critical in marriage because communication is the backbone and the key that starts the engine of our marriages. Those who have mastered this skill in their marriages have fewer problems than those who have not.

When there is a communication breakdown among the players, they start to get confused and lose control of the ball. Double-mindedness, absent-mindedness, or being hesitant to throwing the ball can cause an abrupt losing of the ball or an interception. Full attention is required for execution and the team should be in one accord.

Confusion and running around in marriage is because the husband has not clearly stated the vision. Lack of leadership and planning things together in the home causes confusion. If the husband is not playing his game by directing the traffic in the home, then there is collision everywhere. When there is so much collision in the home then there is no more spending time together. When there is no time for each other, cell phones, Internet, iPad, television and all types of technology starts to compete for our attention. They are after our eyes, ears, touch, hands and our time.

Good communication creates a bond. The husband and wife are free to walk hand in hand, talk, laugh and spend more time together. This is the desire of every married woman. She enjoys it and it makes her feel secure.

When there is no more spending time together, or holding a conversation with each other, something feels the void. Do you want to guess what it is? it is our cell phones. We begin to hold onto our cell phones more than we hold each other's hands.

These gadgets are diverting the real communication between husband and wife. They have become a hiding place when there is no communication between husband and wife.

Look around, especially in restaurants, one will see that people are texting more than talking to each other. We are spending so much time with these gadgets than with each other. We are texting more than verbally communicating. We need to step back and say, "Wait a minute how much time and energy am I spending on the phone than with my husband/wife?"

Do we pay attention to our wife/husband or to our phones? Whom do we pay attention to first, our phone or our husband/wife?

It might sound irrelevant, but these gadgets have taken over the simple face-to-face communication between families. Couples need to feel each other's pain and this can happen when they have more face-to-face interactions. They are not being open to each other about their needs so they take to the movies. Husband and wife are replacing the real communication by watching movies that appeal to their emotions. They are replacing intimacy with what they are looking at. Pornography has taken hold of the young and old minds and it has wrecked many homes. There is always a desire for more. Anything strange to the body always pushes for more.

Dressing has to appeal to the husband according to the movies, or according to the images, he has in his head. All these things are temporary satisfaction, only the husband and wife can satisfy each other permanently. There is more eating out or ordering food than to really cook. The satisfaction of touching, kissing, and cuddling is no more frequent.

Parents get so excited when they see their kids advanced in technology. There is now less communication with the parents and the kids are running around with cell phones and iPads.

These days even the two year olds or even younger are aware of their environment through technology. What the parents are not aware of is that the Internet is babysitting and has become the second parent.

There is nothing wrong with kids learning from the Internet, there has to be a balance. The kids' minds are still growing so they need monitoring. Technology should not take place of face-to-face communication. When there is lack of communication in the home couples will start to drift away from each other and they begin to live like roommates. There has to be time when the family eats around the table and just have fellowship.

Yes, bills could be pressing and husband and wife are working two to three jobs, but still, there has to be time to communicate and find out how each other is doing. We need to cultivate our communication skills and make time for each other if we are going to make our marriages work. Communication is sitting down, plan what works for the family, and still have time for each other.

Notes

_____

_____

_____

_____

_____

_____

_____

_____

_____

_____

_____

_____

_____

_____

_____

_____

_____

_____

_____

Chapter 4

WHEN DOES

COMMUNICATION START?

Communication starts in the womb. God is the first to communicate with his creation. He determines the gender of the child through the seed he has given to the husband; therefore, we should appreciate what God gives us, be it a boy or a girl. Mum and dad begin to communicate with the baby from the time of conception. They express their love by speaking words of love, rubbing, touching and kissing the mother's belly.

The couple begins to prophesy big dreams to their baby before it is even born. The communication that is going on between the parents and the baby, by the time it is born the baby is already acquainted with touch, love, and kisses. When the baby is born the doctors and nurses or mid wives are the first to touch the baby. They make sure that the baby communicates back to them by crying. It is a big concern to doctors and nurses if the baby does not cry.

The crying of the baby is the recognition of new world, from the womb to the real world. It is now a reality check for the baby. The baby's cry is a welcome baby cry, and it is a good sign to those delivering the baby.

After the doctors and nurses are finished examining the baby, they give it to the mother for comfort, love and protection. Relatives and friends get excited as they in turn hold the baby. When the baby is born, touch, love, kisses comfort and protection are not strange to it. It is something she or he has already been experiencing in the womb.

The baby in turn responds by smiling and laughter, which is such joyous communication to the parents.

Therefore, families should make it a ritual to continue touching, kissing and hugging each other even when old. The children never outgrow kisses, hugs and touch.

When there is a lot of hugging, laughing and kissing in the family, it reminds the baby of what had started long back in the womb.

Touching, kissing, holding hands, and cuddling are the bonding that makes the husband and wife come close. It is the best communication a husband and wife can give to each other and to their children.

When there is, no more touching, kissing, cuddling and hugging between husband and wife, it creates a distance between them. Touching, kissing and hugging are irreplaceable. Couples should not be shy; it is a continuation of what started in the womb. It is such a good feeling to cuddle in each other's arms. Husband and wife should establish these attributes from the beginning of their marriage.

Notes

_____

_____

_____

_____

_____

_____

_____

_____

_____

_____

_____

_____

_____

_____

Chapter 5

ENEMIES

OF COMMUNICATION

C ommunication is a skill. We have to develop strong positive skills in order to counteract the negative energies that surround us. The main component in communication is more listening and less talking.

When both of us (husband and wife) are talking to and at each other at the same time, then it is more than likely that no one is listening. Communication needs a lot of listening.

Couples have a tendency of taking each other for granted sometimes. We do not listen to what the other is saying and that gets us in trouble. We have to force ourselves to listen. We need to interpret correctly, what we would have heard, not what we think we heard. The best way to avoid assumptions is to repeat what you just heard or you think you heard to your spouse. Most of the time we regret our actions because we did not take time to listen to what the other was saying. All we did was jump to conclusions.

Let us say there was an intense argument, and the wife gave in or the husband gave in, that did not mean the issue was resolved. What happened here is that the husband or the wife took to a silence factor. The silence factor can be a blessing or a curse. Mostly it is an internalized volcano, which can erupt unexpectedly. Of course, there are times that we have to give each other space, but when silence factor becomes a weapon then it is now an enemy to communication.

When there is a communication breakdown, it creates a void. Either the phone, the Internet, long trips or long hours at work becomes the hiding place. Driving around the neighborhood for hours dreading to go home could be another hiding place.

Unless the couples come to terms with each other, unre-solved issues become the worst enemies to communication. Any time you ask your wife, "what is wrong or what is the matter," and she says, "Nothing," watch out, that is a red flag. There is a whole lot of a conversation going on in her heart and mind that she does not even know what to say at that moment, so all she can say is NOTHING.

Ridicule is the worst enemy of communication between a husband and a wife. It makes the wife or husband feel small or worthless. What we say to each other either builds or breaks us down. Our insecurities hide behind ridicule. The words we say without paying attention hurt the most.

The environment we grew up in either helps us or chal-lenges us to change. If we grew up in families that cursed, and ridiculed, more than likely we are bound to bring those traits into our marriage. Very few people are able to say no to such traits. The majority are still struggling to break away from such bondages. Our environment has the positive and the negative side to it. It becomes our enemy when we be-come an extension of the negativity that hinders us from making prosperous decision as well. I have learnt is that faith or fear comes by hearing.

What we are constantly saying to each other drives a wedge between us or draws us closer. When we do not talk to each other but talk at each other that bring resentment. Resentment creates a wedge that the couple might be physically together and yet miles apart in their minds.

We have to make a choice whether to continue the negativity we learnt or the positivity we want. Are we to continue with the curse or break the curse? We have to be real to self.

"It *takes a while to change a behavior that one thinks is normal to them.*"

In some cultures, they believe that the husband should not share important stuff with his wife. There could be genuine reasons for saying that unfortunately it brings resentment between husband and wife. Such counselling brings division in the home. Watch out for those that give you advise which destroys your marriage, they are your enemy.

Husband and wife should have no secret agendas in the home. Such mindset drives your marriage in reverse gear. When there is communication breakdown, isolation and resentment broods in. Isolation and resentment causes staleness in the marriage.

The danger is that when isolation and resentment finds its way into our marriage, we begin to draw apart. It happens gradually and if it goes unnoticed for a long time, the marriage starts to revert to a point of no return.

In order to amend isolation and resentment, the husband and wife have to stop being defensive. They have to admit that they have been hurting each other so badly that it is causing hemorrhaging. The problem with hemorrhaging is that it is not visible from the outside but internalized. If it goes unnoticed, it can cause death.

We have to have compassion and forgiveness towards each other in areas that have caused us to hemorrhage. Remember you are a team routing for each other not against each other. We should avoid toxicity in our marriages.

If our relationship with God is in good standing, the bad things we do to each other will stop because we reverence Him.

"Unless the Lord builds the house, they labor in vain who build it; unless the Lord guards the city, the watchman stays awake in vain."

Psalms 127:1.

Husbands Communicate better when:

- The wife is in full support of the vision
- Offered the opportunity to help or fix the problem.
- There is no fussing, nagging and too much crying.
- He is always looking for a lap he can put his head on
- He does not have to ask for sex from his wife.
- Praise, hugs and kissed makes him feel at home.
- Time alone, quite time, especially after a busy day.
- He is free to express himself.
- There is no ridicule.
- His wife makes sure he has eaten
- His wife makes sure his clothes are clean
- They desire:
- Honor and respect from their wives.
- Love and appreciation on small and big accomplishments
- To be listened to and trusted

<u>Wives communicate better when there is</u>:

- Love, Touch, hugging, and cuddling
- Undivided attention
- Enough time to talk, wives like to talk
- Security and trust
- Faithfulness
- No cheating
- No comparison to some other women
- Provided for
- Clear vision for the home
- Husband takes his role of leadership
- Security
- Protection
- Loved and appreciated
- Not yelled at
- Trusted and appreciated

Exercise:

List your Communication skills.

_____

_____

_____

_____

_____

_____

_____

_____

What are you planning to do in order to improve your communication skills?

_____

_____

_____

_____

_____

_____

_____

_____

Are you secure enough to express your joy and sadness to each other, if not why?

_____

_____

_____

_____

_____

_____

_____

_____

_____

Do you want things resolved now or later?

_____

_____

_____

_____

_____

_____

_____

_____

What causes you stress?

_____

_____

_____

_____

_____

_____

_____

_____

_____

_____

How do you handle stress?

_____

_____

_____

_____

_____

_____

_____

_____

How do you de-stress yourself?

_____

_____

_____

_____

_____

_____

_____

_____

Are you a risk taker?

_____

_____

_____

_____

_____

_____

_____

_____

_____

What are your fears?

_____

_____

_____

_____

_____

_____

_____

_____

Do you struggle to put your point across?

_____

_____

_____

_____

_____

_____

_____

_____

_____

What do you do when you disagree?

_____

_____

_____

_____

_____

_____

_____

When talking to each other what makes you comfortable and uncomfortable?

_____

_____

_____

_____

_____

_____

_____

_____

_____

How do you reward each other for good communication?

_____

_____

_____

_____

_____

_____

_____

Discuss what honor and respect means to you as a couple.

_____

_____

_____

_____

_____

_____

_____

_____

_____

How do you communicate or want your husband or wife to treat you in public and in private?

_____

_____

_____

_____

_____

_____

_____

As a woman, do you respect men or you resent men if so why?

_____

_____

_____

_____

_____

_____

_____

_____

_____

As a man, do you have respect or resent women if so why?

_____

_____

_____

_____

_____

_____

_____

Do you recall any traumatic moments in your life?

_____

_____

_____

_____

_____

_____

_____

_____

_____

Alternatively, where you violated in any way?

_____

_____

_____

_____

_____

_____

_____

_____

_____

What are the behaviors you are noticing that re-semble your family you grew up?

_____

_____

_____

_____

_____

_____

_____

_____

Are you free to discuss about them?

_____

_____

_____

_____

_____

_____

_____

_____

Was there an open door of communication with your parents or relatives?

_____

_____

_____

_____

_____

_____

_____

_____

_____

How did your parents resolve their marital issues?

_____

_____

_____

_____

_____

_____

_____

_____

_____

What type of communication did you have with your siblings are you close or apart if so why and how are you going to resolve it?

_____

_____

_____

_____

_____

_____

_____

Where you hurt by them in word or deed and how are you going to get over it?

_____

_____

_____

_____

_____

_____

_____

_____

In your own silent moment, what did you promise yourself you will and not allow in your marriage?

_____

_____

_____

_____

_____

_____

_____

Chapter 6

SEX

A SILENT COMMUNICATION

S ex is a very interesting and sensitive topic. Gone are the days that people used to be shy when you mention the "S" word. These days' people talk about sex like it is in fashion.

Not just among married couples, but also among teenagers and adults. It used to be sacred but not anymore. Parents are on the watch out because sex images are popping up on different channels day and night.

It is on radio, magazines, Internet, television and even on billboards. Some programs on television are encouraging people to have sex whether married or not for health reasons. Some songs are about dirty sex and these songs are competing for our ears. Sex trafficking is now a business, a way of making money at the expense of someone's body. All this is a violation of the rules and regulations of sex.

So why is sex so popular, and why all this confusion? It is popular because it is sacred. It is so sacred that its purposes have been misunderstood. If you want to understand what sex is all about, here is the answer. Sex is an intimate relationship between a husband and a wife. They have all the rights to having sex. It is a shame if the husband and wife are not enjoying the benefits and pleasure that God gave to them. Husband and wife should never be shy when it comes to having sex.

Married couples are entitled to enjoy each other sexually. Sex is the glue of marriage and couples should look forward to it. God created it and all that God created was good and is still good up to now! There has to be freedom of expression between husband and wife.

It is very unfortunate that there are couples who are not free to talk about sex to each other. They are shy and some are even afraid of each other. If that is the case in your home then sex has become a routine not an enjoyment.

There should be freedom from the beginning of marriage to discuss about sex. Sometimes the way we grew up, or heard about sex, made us feel like it's a secret thing, dirty, sinful and never to be talked about. We have to overlook cultural barriers that make us not so free to talk about sex. We need to iron out all the misconception that we have heard about sex. We need to remove all the myths we have heard about how bad, and secretive sex is.

There is nothing wrong with sex. We need to make up our minds and start enjoying sex as married couples. You do not have to hide or be in the dark to be intimate. Adam and Eve were naked and not shy about it until they sinned. The good news is that Jesus came and dealt with every sin. If the husband and wife are sinning somewhere, then they should feel shy about it otherwise there is nothing wrong in being naked before the one you love and married. Husband and wife are free to be intimate anytime, anywhere they choose to. Sex is for enjoyment.

There could be times that the other is not in the mood then talk about it. We should not be moody about it especially us wives. If there are barriers that are stopping you from enjoying each other sexually, then be open about it and find help. When couples are open to each other it makes them come closer and love each other even more.

When there is reverence for sex then one does not go around sleeping with whomsoever, they will respect their bodies and keep it for each other. Sex outside the perimeters of marriage becomes toxic. Fornication (sex between the unmarried) or adultery (sex done by married person outside their marriage) becomes a trespass. It is like tearing a page from a book; no matter how you try to put it back together, it will never look the same. Whether it is the husband or wife trespassing, there will never be any satisfaction. They will be looking for more at the wrong places. The behavior becomes like that of an addict, always looking for a fix. Sex is not for a fix. It can only be fulfilling when you engage it with the one you love and married. Sex is not for finding someone you can spend the night with, it is a relaxation for those who are married. I am repeating the words married couples (the man and woman) because that is the protocol.

The only time that couples may abstain from sex is when they are fasting and praying and then they come back together so that the enemy does not tempt them the bible says.

It is unfortunate that not every couple is having sex in their home. Couples who should be having fun and enjoying each other sexually are busy depriving each other of the very thing they were looking forward to when they got married. There are quite a number of couples out there, who are suffering in silence in their home because there is no sex.

Couples who go for months without having sex have become roommates. There is nothing interesting between them anymore. Sex that glues them together is no longer there. It might be okay with the wife but not with the husband. He can turn out to be nasty, grouchy and disrespectful.

When there is a good relationship between a husband and wife, sex is not a dread, but a joy with no sense of guilt whatsoever. Most fulfilled couples are intimate.

When couples no longer have an interest in having sex, it creates many problems, it breaches the covenant of marriage. Sex will no longer be a joy but becomes a weapon used against each other. Every time there is an intense argument, it leads to not having sex. Any little problem leads to no sex in the home. It becomes worse when the husband or wife has to beg each other for sex. Such type of life style will bring temptations of infidelity.

If this is happening in your home right now, please find a way to get back together. This is happening in Christian and none Christian homes. Depriving each other of romance, love, intimacy, and sex is a danger to married couples. My friends we are all guilty of this, we have to stop this madness in our homes.

Constantly hurting each other with words or deeds causes a close in among couples. When there are unresolved issues, sex then becomes a duty not a joy. It then becomes cheap when done for wrong reasons. Sex is for relaxation between the husband and his wife. It is their secret life.

They do not go about publishing how they do it, but how they reverence it as a pleasure given by God. I am not a marriage counselor or a sex therapist, I am a married woman who has experienced all these things and I would not want to see anyone go through what I went through ignorantly. I am one of the many voices sounding an alarm to say come this way the other way is too painful and unnecessary. Sex becomes bad when couples engage in it outside the perimeters of marriage.

When there is fear of rejection, molestation, rape or abuse of some sort, it is difficult for some to discuss about it. When discussing with such individuals there has to be an atmosphere of acceptance, not judgmental. Both of you are starting a new adventure in marriage therefore love should be the banner of your marriage. Forget the past, build your marriage, and enjoy each other sexually. Find time to discuss and know each other more and be open to each other.in every area of each other's life.

Avoid communications that drives you away from wanting sex or rather make you lose interest in sex. Cultivate love communication, respect each other and see the best in each other. Be positive about your sex life. Comparing your marriage to someone's marriage brings insecurity.

Therapy is crucial sometimes when couples feel like they cannot help each other. You hear couples say we have been to several therapists and it never helped, please be open for help there are qualified people trained to help in certain areas of life so make appointments and get help.

Wishing your marriage would be like so and so marriage is dangerous because you have no idea what goes on behind closed doors.

Learn from other couples, yes, but build your own marriage. Talk to each other if there were any major surgeries, for example tube ligation, vasectomy, removal of uterus and many more.

"I wish I had known syndrome is a damaging thought in marriage; it will eat you up and make you miserable in your marriage."

When couples are open with each other, even sex is very easy and enjoyable. Tension comes when there is uncertainty. Where there is doubt and suspicion between the husband and wife sex life deteriorates. The wife is on the edge as well as the husband. Trust is the foundation of marriage. Do not be afraid to ask each other anything that is on your heart, be it current issues or previous issues. This is where communication is very vital. Bad movies, masturbation and pornography are the enemies of marriage. They get you hooked, and then leave you an addict. Addictions are hard to break because an evil spirit drives them. There is no way one can satisfy an evil spirit, it is a strange thing to the body.

When the body is broken down there is no more sense of guilt, the alarm system inside you is silenced and bad stuff look normal.

People who have been involved in these weird acts tell you that it always looked like an innocent thing to do until they were addicted.

If you start your relationship on truthfulness, then there is no need to prove anything to each other all the time. However, if you start your marriage on a lie then you have a lot to work on. You have to remember what you said yesterday, which is difficult if it was a lie.

We should not keep score of how many times we had sex it is a life style. However, if there are continuous excuses from both sides of not having sex then it drives the relationship into a bad mode. Lack of communication takes away the desire of intimacy between husband and wife. They say men think of sex more than women do. That could be true and not true. When there is good communication between husband and wife, you think more on sex. You want to be close to each other in every area.

Women tend to lose desire for sex because we operate according to our feelings. If our feelings are hurt all the time, we just shut off sexually. We begin to think like, "How can I sleep with a man who does not love me?" Sex to women is an expression of love.

It means that you are there for me and respect me. Women need more touch and more conversation. Wives want to know that they are wanted. Sex to them should not be a routine or a job. It should be an attraction driven by a free desire. When the husband forces sex on his wife, it physically hurts her. It just feels like your husband is rapping you. Intimacy should be enjoyable between a husband and wife. It all boils down to how we communicate and desire to meet each other's needs.

There should be a sense of respect and not condemnation. There has to be a freedom of expression, no hang-ups or pointing of a finger. Husbands/wives should not feel good when they put each other down or feel superior to the other. That is a sign of insecurity. Lack of wisdom, knowledge and understanding of each other causes such behaviors. When we get married, we should help each other to be even much better than we found each other. We should look at each other with the eye of love not hatred. When we treat each other with respect sex becomes easy and enjoyable. Couples have to help each other on which contraceptives is best for them. Every woman is different so husband and wife should help each other to see what works for them.

When a wife puts on weight, eventually it affects her self-esteem. It makes it worse when the husband starts to put pressure on the wife to lose weight. It stresses the wife out. She begins to withdraw; and she loses hope in losing weight the best remedy is for the husband to understand that the wife already feels bad and all she wants is her husband to not condemn, but to help her.

Some women might have had surgery when they had the baby so they are always struggling with their bodies. Be open to talk to each other so that there is no hurting of each other's feelings. I remember there was a time my husband wanted me to put on weight. I had never seen anything wrong with me being skinny until he said that.

All of a sudden, my confidence and self-esteem went down the drain. I felt so inadequate. I began to think like, oh...well...that is why you have been treating me like this and that because you need more flesh to hold onto. I tried to act as if it did not bother me but in secret, it did. I began to be miserable and slowly I lost interest in having sex. We could be intimate but my mind would be drifting away all the time. I thought I was no fit for him anymore.

I began to think maybe there is a fat woman out there he wants me to be like and it was not a good place for me to be.

Husband and wife can deplete each other by words and action. What we say to each other matters the most.

I started praying to God to make me fat, I twisted his arm to make me fat and for sure, God answered my prayer. I began to gain weight and my husband began to notice it and I thought now he was going to be happy because I was getting bigger. He was for some time, and then one day he said, "I think you need to lose weight for your health." I thought, "Forget you", I am like this because you wanted me fat, now I am fat you telling me to lose weight again! "Forget you!" I became rebellious even though at the back of my mind I knew what he said was true.

Instead of us drawing closer, we were drawing apart and the sex life was in jeopardy as well. I realized that when it comes to my health I should never have ever put on weight in the first place. I caused this on myself I knew it had some consequences but because I wanted to please my husband. I went ahead and did it. Now I am on a regime to lose weight but this is because I want to not because my husband said so. Sometimes God allows things to happen so we learn a lesson.

Please do not do what I did, that was not true love but false love. In a capsule, Sex is relational. Sex is not lustful. Lust is instant gratification.

When the husband and wife improve on their relationship, the rest will fall in place. Watch how you talk to each other. Words are easy to say, but hard to take back. Words and actions either break you or make you.

Women process words repeatedly, it is like a rewind, and the record keeps on playing. It takes time for women to let go of the pain caused by words, they begin to ask so what did he mean by saying this; we try to get an answer to no avail.

I would recommend for husbands to be careful on how they talk to their wives to have an enjoyable sex life. When an argument occurs, give each other time to recuperate, this stops the closing in. Plan a gateway with your wife it refreshes the marriage. Remember sex is the glue that keeps the marriage together.

Exercise:

How is your sex life in your home?

_____

_____

_____

_____

_____

_____

Have you been open to discuss about your previous sexual encounters before marriage if there were any?

_____

_____

_____

_____

_____

_____

Do you feel vulnerable when you try to be open to each other?

_____

_____

_____

_____

_____

_____

_____

_____

Are you strong enough to meet with the ex-boyfriend or ex-girlfriend who you know was intimate with your wife or husband?

_____

_____

_____

_____

_____

_____

_____

Do you look forward to being intimate with your husband/wife or you resent it?

_____

_____

_____

_____

_____

_____

_____

_____

_____

_____

_____

_____

_____

_____

_____

_____

_____

_____

_____

What are the major causes of you resenting intimacy with your wife or husband?

<u>Choose from the list below</u>.

- Rejection
- Needs not met physically mentally and spiritually
- No communication
- Disrespect and ridicule
- Embarrassment
- Disrespect from family friends
- Fear
- Pain, shy
- Cheating
- Lying
- Health issues
- Un-forgiveness
- Other

When there is no sex between husband and wife, isolation begins. Make a list of all you feel has made you to isolate.

Choose from the list below.

- Fear of hurt
- Rejection
- Vulnerability
- Hopelessness
- Insecurity
- Aloneness
- Low self-esteem
- Pride
- Does not trust

How does it affect you when you deprive each other sexually?

_____

_____

_____

_____

_____

_____

_____

_____

What is the remedy for change?

_____

_____

_____

_____

_____

_____

_____

_____

_____

_____

Notes

_____

_____

_____

_____

_____

_____

_____

_____

_____

_____

_____

_____

_____

_____

_____

_____

_____

_____

_____

_____

Chapter 7

THE WIFE'S ROLE

A wife is a nurturer, caretaker and has to understand her role very well. She understands that she is not the head of the house, but a helper with a lap for her husband to lay and rest on. It is her position that matters the most, not her condition. She is single minded and she carries herself with dignity. She is on display for her own husband. Her whole body attracts and satisfies her own husband. Her curves are just for him. in addition, she submits to her own husband.

I have mentioned _own husband_ several times because there should not be a mix up on whom the wife should submit. We respect other men but submission is for our husbands.

What is submission? There is quite a lot of misunderstanding when we talk about submission. Submission is not a master slave mentality. The wife gives her willful act to her husband. She respects and honors her husband.

It is very easy to submit where there is love and respect. If you take your wife by the hand and lead her to greener pastures, submission is very easy. You become her lord, why, because you are exercising your role as her leader. A wife delights in her husband taking his leadership role. The bible also talks about the husband and wife submitting one to another. Love is the key that opens the treasure box of submission.

God saw that Adam needed a wife to take away his aloneness, so he went ahead and created Eve for him. He created her from his rib. She came from Adam's side not from behind. She enjoys equal rights in her man's life. The rib cage protects our vital organs; therefore, she as a rib also is protective of what is hers. She is like surveillance light.

When she operates fully in her domain, she is neither jealous nor overprotective. She is one flesh with her husband and her husband cleaves to her. She simply takes care of what is hers in wisdom. She works hand in hand with her husband. She can engage herself in so many things at one time. She is multi-tasked. She is a useful helper to her husband. Her position is that she is well able to help her husband in whatever capacity he needs help. She is not a door mate, neither abusive but is there to be a help fit for her husband.

A wife has to catch the vision as the husband explains it to her. Without a vision, the family perishes. She prays and continuously reminds her husband of his purpose. The wife can build or bring down her house, with her own hands. Her words are to bless her husband and not to bring him down. She should not bring shame to her husband. She graces herself with love, joy, peace and happiness.

She knows who she is and she walks in favor with God and favor with people. She is free with people, chooses who comes close to her, and knows who is for real and who is not. She can discern when things are not well with her husband and always ready to help.

She can smell a rat from far because that is her position to stop the storm and bring stability in the home. Anything that violates oneness in her home she will come against it. The wife is full of compassion, prays, gives and teaches her kids to fear God. Her thoughts about her husband are to do him good all the days of his life. She thrives in his support, praise, love and protection. Her husband protects and encourages her. When given an opportunity she is able to buy land and plants vineyards, she is a businessperson and an entrepreneur. Her husband and family call her blessed.

Her husband carries himself with confidence knowing that his wife loves him. She makes him feel like a king and loves him with true love. She does not humiliate her husband but honors her husband. She is always ready to support her husband and she is a truthful person. She makes sure the house is clean, cooks for the family and makes sure both leave the house well groomed. She is a friend indeed to her husband. She harnesses her spirit and she carries herself with dignity. Steel waters run deep! She knows when to open her mouth and when to shut it. Her husband feels at home and looks forward to coming home to a welcoming wife. She is satisfied to be married to her husband. She is confident and does not look for affirmation from other men.

Her bedroom is a place of rest, a sanctuary of joy, peace and happiness. It is a room of pleasure and not a courtroom, a place of peace and tranquility. She creates a good atmosphere for her bedroom. in addition, finds a place other than her bedroom for her and her husband to resolve their issues.

Most married women are not operating in their maximum capacity because they are married to men who do not know or appreciate what God has given them. When the wife is discouraged, she loses her sense of living and everything around her starts to deteriorate.

The husband has to understand that the wife can get tired. If all she is doing is giving, giving, and nothing in return, she will soon lose the momentum. Loving and relieving her of her day today chores fills her tank. If she runs on empty for a long time, she breaks down. Husbands, take your wives to a higher dimension than you found her. When you do that, not only are you taking care of a soul but the favor of God will start operating in your life even more.

"He who finds a wife finds a good thing and obtains favor with God." Proverbs 18:22.

Characteristics that take away from the wife:

- Busy body and gossiper
- Disrespect, dirty house, dirty children, and dirty herself.
- Loud mouth, Loves to sin, Jealous and envious
- Tells everything about her home issues to everyone.
- Accusing, unappreciative, always nagging.
- Lazy, and has an excuse for everything.
- Does not like the things of God
- Always right and everybody else wrong
- Does not listen
- Angry and bickering
- Hateful Home wrecker, spending money unnecessarily
- Fights her husband
- Love ancestral and Idol worship.
- Smokes and drinks. Cheats on her husband

Discuss what you have done right as a wife and what needs to be improved

_____

_____

_____

_____

_____

_____

_____

_____

_____

_____

_____

_____

_____

_____

_____

_____

_____

_____

List your strengths and weaknesses

_____

_____

_____

_____

_____

_____

_____

_____

_____

_____

_____

_____

_____

_____

_____

_____

_____

_____

Chapter 8

THE HUSBAND'S ROLE

Husbands are very important and very intelligent. When God has instructions for the family, he communicates with the husband. It does not matter whether he is a man of big stature or of a small stature, his position matters the most than the outside looks. He has to hear from God. His position is more important than his condition. We should address our husbands from their positions rather than their conditions. It is a dangerous thing for a husband to let the wife lead the home because that is not her position.

Every man is born with leadership qualities. All they need to do is to develop raw materials of leadership within them. If a man does not want to work then he is neglecting his position.

The husband receives instructions from God and his position is that of true strength, father, and provider.

Husbands are well able to provide and protect. Protection and provision is the language one hears from most husbands. His strength is for protection and not for abuse. His wife is his glory, and he needs a wife who encourages him even if it does not make sense sometimes.

He is the head and the high priest of his home. When Adam was tending the garden, God gave him the intelligence to name all the animal kingdom. He received specific instructions on which tree to eat from and not to eat. That is why when they ate of the forbidden fruit God called Adam not Eve. Therefore, there should never be words like, "Oh! He is dull, or he does not know anything." He is well able to carry on the affairs of his home.

The husband has two critical positions in life. He is a husband and a father. He is the first father figure to his children and their first line of defense.

He protects his children, and is required to know how to direct the traffic of his household. He is at peace when he knows that his family loves and believes in him. His worst enemies are ridicule and disrespect whether in private or in secret. Respect, praise and honor are the fuel, which drives him to do more. A man who fears God does not entangle himself with evil things.

Husbands do not want their ego ruffled; they want to be in charge all the time. He thinks in terms of fixing things, meaning in his mind he is continuously looking for ways to make things better. He gets motivated when his wife celebrates, and appreciates him even on small achievements. Therefore, the wife has to encourage and stand by her husband when life is good and not so good.

When the wife is always asking, "Where are we going and what is the plan?" It is because the husband has not clarified the vision to his wife.

The husband should present the vision in such a way that the family buys into it without any doubt. When the family buys into the vision, together they create a final plan that welcomes new information making them to realign with the environment they are in.

Vision always encounters new information that requires revisiting the dream in the light of new demands.

It is easier for the family to accept the vision when the husband knows how to execute it.

Many times wives have the impression that husbands do not care simply because they do not feel empathy from them. That is not the case, husbands like to think things through and is not as emotional as their wives are. They can only do one task at a time. Once they make up their mind, they are risk takers.

In general, the husband thinks and talks about long-term plans. What he needs to do is to assure his wife that he cares about the present situation as well. His hands are for protection not for physical abuse. His mouth is for building and not for destroying. He is a man of honor and integrity. He tells the truth, lives a life of honesty and trustworthy. He loves his wife and his children. Hand in hand, he walks with his wife.

The husband should make sure that his wife feels secure and that she always knows that her husband has her back. He leads the home by example.

Remember, opposites attract therefore the husband and wife should celebrate their differences. The problem comes when we try to mold each other into what we want. Couples should complement each other. In this case, the husband should lead with confidence even if he makes mistakes sometimes.

He does not rule his family with an iron feast but leads like a shepherd leads the sheep and nurses the lambs. The husband should leave an inheritance for his children's children.

Wealth and riches are in his house. He finds land and builds his estate. Together with his wife, they raise their children and guide them. He sets aside funds for the children's education and provides for their future.

A family that puts God first is an honorable family.

"By humility and fear of the Lord are riches and honor and life." Proverbs 22:4.

Characteristics that take away from the husband:

- Abuse
- Hitting
- Laziness
- Infidelity
- Lying
- Wanting the wife to take care of the family
- Disrespectful
- Double minded
- Demeaning
- Threatens
- Always his way
- Secret life
- Hides money
- Secretly taking care of his children with other wives
- Concubines

Discuss what you have done right and what needs to be improved.

_____

_____

_____

_____

_____

_____

_____

_____

What is your way forward from today as a high priest and provider of your home?

_____

_____

_____

_____

_____

_____

_____

_____

_____

What are your weaknesses and your strengths?

_____

_____

_____

_____

_____

_____

_____

_____

_____

_____

_____

_____

_____

_____

_____

_____

Chapter 9

DO I HAVE TO GET MARRIED TO BE HAPPY?

Marriage is a choice. We cover ground as we go. I have heard people say if marriage is like so and so marriage, then I would rather stay single. They say that with a passion, why, because they have observes an unpleasant marriage. They might right, but that is not how marriage should be. When the relationship becomes toxic, then it is no longer a marriage, it is now a poison and it can kill.

Not every marriage is toxic; there are couples out there who have figured it out on how to enjoy a pleasant marriage. Therefore, before you can make any conclusions on one or two toxic marriages look out for the ten who are really having a blast in their marriages. In marriage, we are continuously learning and discovering the good, the bad and the ugly about each other, and yet willing to change for the best of our marriages. There has to be a singleness of mind. If one is a double-minded person, then nothing comes to fruition.

We do not have to get married in order to be happy. One gets married because he/she is already a happy person! Happiness is before and after marriage. The pillars of marriage are joy, peace and happiness. A happy individual creates a happy marriage.

Miserable individuals bring misery into their marriages. They spend their married life wishing they had never been married. They have a mindset of could have, would have, and should have. This type of an individual is hard to please. Marriage is a commitment. They are looking for someone to make them happy. Being so needy and miserable, it drains the other partner.

Can one make lemonade out of the bitterness of their marriage? You cannot sign up for a team and say I just want to be here for a week or so, and if it does not work then I quit. They will tell you that you are out of your mind; we do not play the game that way here. We do not get married to see if it works. It is a commitment. We get out of it what we invest in it.

Our life in marriage will progress through several dimensions; from the looks and show off, to parenting and hustling for a better life. The process of marriage then changes to deeper relationship and understanding of family priorities. The development of the marriage challenges the couple to become a solid family and the definition of beauty then becomes that of the heart, which is what matters in marriage.

Out of the abundance of the heart the mouth speaks. Happiness is your personality and you bring that with you into your marriage. Marriage will not make you happy but will magnify your happiness.

Notes

Chapter 10

DOES MARRIAGE REALLY WORK?

Marriage works when we work it. It works when we are willing to play the game for each other and not against each other. Discipline is the key. It intrigues me that God blessed marriage before He blessed the Church. It is important to Him therefore it must be important to us. *"Through wisdom a house is built, and by understanding it is established, by knowledge the rooms are filled with all precious and pleasant riches."* *Proverbs 24:3-4.*

Wisdom is the principle thing in marriage. We have to learn to be team players. Saying empty and hurtful words at and to each other brings negative results.

"Words are like an echo; they still make noise in a slow motion after you have spoken them. They travel so fast, hit the hardest, and leave a residue."

The tongue is unruly and difficult to tame. We have to watch what we say to each other as married couples. Speak and act positively, mean what you say and say what you mean. Go where you are celebrated, not tolerated. We have heard this saying in conferences and in different meetings. What does it really mean? It means that when people celebrate you, for whom you are, and then you are capable of producing more.

When there is disrespect in marriage; then there is not much production. Couples should complement each other all the time. Everyone in this universe wants to be recognized. When the husband and wife see value in each other then they will respect and honor each other. They become fruitful in everything they do together. Can you pinpoint when the tide began to turn in your marriage?

When you decide to go for a bike ride with your husband and you realize that there is a curve ahead of you, if you do not lean over, you are more than likely to fall off the bike. One has to know when to lean over when riding the bike of marriage; otherwise, you are more than likely to fall off the bike of marriage.

If you cannot trace the footsteps of your marriage any longer, that could be when the tide started. The tide is issues that popped up and were never resolved. Overlooking issues and assuming everything to be okay, is not a way to move forward. Sometimes one has to get the bull by the horns. Confrontation is not easy but couples have to be bold enough to confront these issues in love, so that they can move on to the next level.

When we learn how to separated issues from who we are, then we have a greater insight on how to face adversity when it comes against our marriages. Just say to yourself, "I have been through this before, there is nothing new about this it will soon pass." Learn to ride on the eye of the storm.

Remember in order to win the game, there has to be a lot of practicing, hustling and then follows a touchdown. One has to be mentally prepared and stick to the rules.

Some quit because of the game's intensity. How bad do you want it? It is all up to the two of you, the husband and wife. There is always a light at the end of the tunnel. During practice, some team members are injured and they have to sit on the bench until healed. The same applies to marriage; sometimes we say things and do things that hurt each other. Therefore, we have to give each other time to heal. Avoid words like, 'get over it', or 'you are a cry baby.' People react differently to pain and discouragement. Marriage is not a one size fits all kind of a thing.

Follow your own blueprint and create the marriage that works for you. Love and respect are the most important elements in marriage. The material things that we bring into the marriage do not determine if the marriage is going to be a great marriage or not. How we build the foundation of our marriages is what determines the outcome. Our solid rock is Jesus and he is the chief cornerstone of our marriage.

Our husbands are our quarterbacks, point guards, or team captains. Our purpose as wives is to see to it that our husbands are healthy enough to stay in the game. Words of respect and honor are the best nutrition to our husbands.

Remember the wife is the wide receiver and she is always running to a place of receiving the ball. Thinking fast and making fast decisions are a requirement for a quarterback. If he is too slow to make decisions, he becomes a target for tackling. The husband is the quarterback of his family he has to be able to make sound decisions of his family. If communication is uncoordinated then he might throw the ball when the wife cannot sprint enough to catch the ball and make a touchdown. Couples have to be willing to talk about the past, present and future. Fear, anxiety, depression, idol worship, poverty, riches, anger, hatred, animosity and un-forgiveness, are some of the things that we bring in our marriages. There should be a freedom of expression in these areas of life between husband and wife without fear.

Ask each other why we act the way we do. If its anger, we should deal with the root cause. Anger is rooted mainly in rejection. Find out what it is that caused one to feel rejected. A happy marriage is the greatest thing you can give to each other. You grow and discover a lot about each other and can add many good years to your life if you are willing to work at it. Marriage works when both parties agree most of the time, and willing to work out their differences. Remember marriage is two imperfect people working towards perfection.

Notes

_____

_____

_____

_____

_____

_____

_____

_____

_____

_____

_____

_____

_____

_____

_____

_____

Chapter 11

WHAT ARE THE BENEFITS OF MARRIAGE?

Two is better than one. One chases a thousand and two chases ten thousand. Married couples become a solid team that cannot be broken. Husband and wife get to spend the rest of their lives together, loving each other with no reservations. They get to share their bodies freely, guiltless and with no shame. He who finds a wife finds a good thing and has favor with God. The husband becomes the protector of his family and there is a tendency of living long among <u>loving</u> couples.

It gets easier tackling issues of life together as a married couple. The financial status tends to increase when married that is if you are married to a man who wants to work. There are benefits of tax breaks depending on how much both of you will have made. Society has a different look at married people than single there is sort of a respect somehow.

What have you benefited from your marriage?

_____

_____

_____

_____

_____

_____

_____

_____

_____

_____

_____

Chapter 12

REKINDLING YOUR LOVE

We should never forget the day we set eyes on each other and how it felt. I have heard people say love is not a feeling, I think it is to an extent. I felt it when I set eyes on my fiancé who is now my husband. It is healthy to revisit you good olden days. It will bring you back to the sanity that you are still the same person and can still love as before and ever better. If you have your old pictures, bring them out and if possible, visit the places you went when in courtship. Take time to laugh. Talk about the good and the bad of that courtship journey.

Remember that aunt or uncle or whoever it was who just wanted to make things difficult and laugh about it. Remind each other of the day you held hands kissed and went for lunch if you did.

Re-Visit Exercise:

What steps did you take to win her or him?

_____

_____

_____

_____

_____

How did you find each other?

_____

_____

_____

_____

_____

Who proposed first?

_____

_____

_____

_____

_____

_____

_____

_____

_____

What attracted you to her?

_____

_____

_____

_____

_____

_____

_____

_____

_____

What attracted you to him?

_____

_____

_____

_____

_____

_____

_____

_____

_____

How did you introduce her/him to the parents and what was their response?

_____

_____

_____

_____

_____

_____

_____

_____

How was your honeymoon if you had one?

_____

_____

_____

_____

_____

_____

_____

_____

What is it that still draws you to each other?

_____

_____

_____

_____

_____

_____

_____

_____

_____

What draws you apart?

_____

_____

_____

_____

_____

_____

_____

_____

If you were to start, all over what would you do and not do?

_____

_____

_____

_____

_____

_____

Chapter 13

THE BATTLE OF CHOICE

Not every couple has a privilege of finding each other. People interpret and experience marriage in different ways. Some cultures do not allow their children to marry outside their families. Young girls in other cultures have arranged marriages. They go to an old man's house stay there until they are mature enough to be married. These girls have no choice but to accept it. These arranged marriages force women to love someone they do not like.

In their minds, they are imagining how it could have been if they had married the man, they loved. Most marital problems are because of things like this.

Some of these girls manage to break off and find the love of their life but how about those who do not. Can you imagine learning to love the man you never loved in the first place? This is going on in other cultures.

Jacob in the bible struggled in his marriage because his father in-law gave him Leah instead of Rachel. We see constant struggle in Jacob's marriage because of what his father-in-law did. Leah thought maybe Jacob would love her by having kids but that was not the issue, Jacob loved Rachel.

Rule of thumb; marry the one you love not who they want you to marry if possible. This will give you peace of mind and there will not be a blaming game when issues of life pop up. How you build, your house depends on both of you. I am going to share with you two stories that show that there is a battle of choice when it comes to marriage. Marriage is a mixture of culture and beliefs.

The dowry issue

We all come from different cultures and beliefs. In my culture there has to be a dowry paid by the bridegroom for his groom. Dowry is the charges the parents of the groom charge the bridegroom in order to marry their daughter.

Most bridegrooms struggle to come up with the correct amount of these required charges. The groom does not have much to say when it comes to the decisions her parents and her relatives charge. This is the traditional marriage before the white wedding.

So many factors determine how much is for dowry. If the girl is a virgin or educated and has a good career, the price goes up. There are also other charges like buying the clothes for the wife's parents and a certain number of cows. This is the day the wife's parents become rich within a moment. I am not here to put down any cultural practice there are pros and cons to this practice. Many bridegrooms struggle to come up with the money and it causes a postponement in marriage.

Some of the husbands treat their wives like purchased property because of the dowry they paid. The wife has to endure the abuse of her husband because of the dowry. Some parents charge so much and they have no idea of the after math. Because of this, there are reports of domestic violence at go unaccounted for because the wife is afraid to vocalize it.

It becomes worse when the couple relocates to a foreign land. Most couples become alone and lonely because they left their families to live abroad and nobody really knows what is going on in that family. Abuse becomes evident. The life style is in isolation and abuse becomes evident.

Arranged marriages

I was just waiting to go to class, passing time when I started talking to this girl who had just travelled from overseas to be with her husband. I asked her where her husband was and she said he was coming later for his class as well.

As we continued talking and laughing I asked her where they had met, and she said she had never met him in person.

All she had was a picture of him. Her parents arranged the marriage and her coming to America was her first time to meet him.

I asked her if she loved the person, and she said she was scared at first but was learning how to love him. I asked her if she had any relatives here and she said she did not and was very lonely and she missed her twin sister.

I assured her that anytime she sees me and wants to visit was okay with me. She was very excited and at that moment, her husband walked in. She introduced me to him, and they left. As a mother, I began to think of how I could help her but I was helpless. I hope she is okay.

After school, another day I had called an Uber (a taxi) to pick me up from College and on my way home the person started asking me where I was from. When I told him, he sounded interested in carrying on the conversation. I will call him James (not his real name)

James, "Oh...I almost married a girl from your country."

Me, "So what stopped you?"

James; "My parents and her parents did not approve of my church so we had to go separate ways."

Me, "where is she now and how long did you date?" He answered, "Two years, she went abroad."

Me, "Do you still keep in touch?"

James; "Yes as a matter of fact I have just come from seeing her because she had asked me to bring her some stuff from here. We still friends."

Me, "Do you have a girlfriend now?"

James; "Yes my parents arranged for me to see this other girl and I am learning to love her but the one I love is the one overseas the problem is I don't want to disappoint my parents or to be rejected by all of my relatives".

Me, "All I can say to you is you have to marry the woman you love, anyway I am going to pray for you to make the right decision."

He started laughing but I could sense the uneasiness in his voice. What do you do in such cases and how do you help such marriages? When I got home, I said good-bye to him and got out of the car. I just had a sense of sadness as I got into my house because I wanted this person to marry the girl he loved. I have to think of how many people were marrying against their own will, and how do you help such marriages.

In order for marriage to work, you have to marry the one you love. Marriage should be an individual's right to choose one's life partner and friend. You marry for yourself and you should live with the consequences of your choice. Let us not be quick to point a finger or make our own conclusions when we see someone struggling in his or her marriage. Instead, we should seek to understand how we could give a genuine helping hand. This whole experience I had with these two individuals made me think of how some people are so deceived to think their marriage is better than so and so. If it were you in such a situation how would you handle it   marriage then becomes complicated in such scenarios. Comparing our marriages with someone else marriage brings strife in the home and it is not necessary. In my language we a proverb that says, "What covers the houses are roofs", meaning roofs look the same but what goes on under those roofs is your guess and my guess.

People always put their best foot forward. Wishing your husband was like your neighbor, or your wife was as the woman down the street is a waste of time and energy. We need to surround our marriages with people who love to be married and value morals and principles of marriage. You become whom you hang around.

Marriage is enjoyable when God is the center. We learn from others whilst we are working our own marriages. When helping couples it is always good to find out more information before we make our own conclusions. What we might think could be the cause of problems in someone's marriage, might be totally a different thing all together.

Exercise:

Discuss what these words mean to you as a couple.

Kissing and holding hands

_____

_____

_____

_____

_____

_____

Touch

_____

_____

_____

_____

_____

_____

Love, joy, peace, and happiness.

_____

_____

_____

_____

_____

_____

_____

_____

_____

_____

_____

Do you feel pressured or you feel free to love your spouse?

_____

_____

_____

_____

_____

_____

_____

Do you feel it is the wife's duty to do all the chores or you are willing to help? When do you feel you should help?

_____

_____

_____

_____

_____

_____

_____

_____

Chapter 14

FINANCES

Let the poor say I am rich and let the weak say I am strong. What we say is what starts the engine of our life. Whatever we settle for is what we get. If all we talk about is poverty, lack, need and want it will eventually happen. It is a mindset. Wherever you park your mind that is where it is going to remain. As a man thinks so is he. The moment we renew our minds and start talking about riches and good life, before time we will be experiencing it. We are a sum total of what we think, say and act.

We have to call those things, which are not as though they are, the bible says. Poverty is not from God. It does not matter how much we try to justify it. Prosperity is not a name it or claim it as per say, it is a life style. It hurts to be poor; starting your day thinking on how you are going to make it is overwhelming. It is frustrating and painful to live a life of poverty.

One can be so poor that they cannot pay attention. To be poor is when you find yourself wishing and not being able to provide or do anything for yourself and those around you. It can also be that of having money and yet living an undisciplined life. Money answers all things the bible says. Poverty can also be having all the money and yet alone, no peace and suicidal. Stinginess leads to poverty as well. There are extremes on both ends.

Our hands are for working and not for begging. We reap what we sow, and whatever we put our hands to do it prospers. God gives us power to gain wealth. He wants us to have both wealth and riches. Wealth and riches are in the house of the righteous. We do not prosper sitting down and hopping some money is going to drop from heaven. One has to have a strategy on how they are going to make it in life.

"Through wisdom a house is built and by understanding it is established by knowledge the rooms are filled with all precious and pleasant riches."

Proverbs 24:3-6.

In order to prosper one has to visualize and bring their mind to believe that there is nothing wrong in having money. What is wrong is money having us. I had to tell myself this repeatedly, until I believed that there was nothing wrong with having money. I would get money, and then I would give it away, get it again, and then give it away. I had a wrong teaching on giving. We should not give out of impulse, or we heard that someone gave so much and he or she prospered. Give because you know that in your heart you have to give. There is nothing wrong in giving but one has to know how to give to self as well.

I remember when I was growing up; almost every day there would be women sitting by the roadside selling vegetables. They looked like they did not have any money at all and yet at the end of the day they would go home with pockets full of money. What I failed to understand was the exchange of commodity that was happening between the two. They were selling, we were buying, and we were both profiting.

If there is lack of understanding on how to prosper, take time to learn from books, classes, seminars, even your peers who are well versed in prosperity.

Do something to improve in this area of your life. The husband and wife should plan and agree on their monetary issues. There are families that are not open to each other about money. The husband hides money from his wife and vice versa, this type of lifestyle leads to poverty. Money is a blessing in the home when there is openness about it. Most marriages break up because of lack of finances. The wife should not take the burden of providing for the family. It should never be at any point in time that a wife should worry about the provision of the family.

The husband takes care of the family financially. If he cannot provide for his family then he is worse than an infidel the bible says. In case of looking for a job, then the husband has to be aggressiveness about it. It is in the DNA of the husband to till the ground and take care of his family. The wife is a helper not a provider.

Not finding a job should not be a permanent excuse for the husband for not taking care of his family.

The family gets motivated to pitch in when they see dad working and providing for the family. The wife should not put down her husband because her job pays her more than her husband does.

If the wife loves her husband, she will find ways to help him rather than looking down on him because she gets more money than he does.

Respect and honor between husband and wife brings peace in the home. There should never be secret money stashed in the bank somewhere or secret businesses somewhere everything should be in the open. Husband and a wife should agree on their personal accounts. In the case of giving the wife, money to take care of the home, the husband should not look at it like an allowance. Allowance is for children. The husband and wife can have separate accounts for emergency but everything should be in the open.

Hiding things or agendas from each other create mistrust and suspicion. Trust is a big word to the wife. Unity builds the home; mistrust breaks the home. His money is hers too or vice versa. The husband and wife should have the freedom of sharing their money and prosper together.

Exercise:

What do you understand about money?

_____

_____

_____

How are you going to multiply your money?

_____

_____

_____

_____

_____

How much debt do you have?

_____

_____

_____

_____

_____

How much do you understand about; investments, mutual funds, gold, forex trading, real estate etc.

_____

_____

_____

_____

_____

_____

_____

_____

_____

_____

_____

_____

_____

_____

_____

_____

_____

Notes

Chapter 15

HOW DO WE TREAT OUR FRIENDS?

Our friends mean a lot to us. Some of our friends we grew up with, some we met in college at work and some when we got married. We should always cherish our friendships. We make friends everywhere we go. Friendship reunions are very healthy and should be encouraged. We should encourage our spouses to continue friendship with their good friends. Good friends build but bad friends break up the marriage. Friends should build and not bring division in marriage.

Some wives or husbands are so possessive they do not even want their spouse to socialize with others. Unless there are genuine reasons, such insecurity will put each other in bondage. We have to remember we met each other when we had friends already. If we had bad friends, then we should be open to good friends and have fun. Marriage should be fun not bondage. All we need to do is let our friends know their limits in our homes. Friends have to be conscious of the rules of the home and not impose their own rules. My closest friend is now my husband and none of our friends should separate us. The wife has to know who her husband's friends are and the husband has to know who his wife's friends are as well.

Be open to discuss with your wife or husband if you feel uncomfortable with some of the friends. There are no secret dealings with friends. Friendship with ex-girlfriends or ex-boyfriends is a sensitive one and should not be encouraged. If there is disrespect from either side of friends then they have to go. Some friends are agents of the enemy. A friend becomes an enemy when he or she becomes attracted to your husband or wife. She is no more a friend but a home wrecker. Some friends are true friends, so recognize them. If you want friends, show yourself friendly.

Exercise:

What are the pros of your friends?

_____

_____

_____

_____

_____

_____

_____

_____

_____

_____

_____

_____

_____

_____

_____

_____

What are the cons of your friends?

_____

_____

_____

_____

_____

_____

_____

_____

_____

_____

_____

_____

_____

_____

_____

_____

Chapter 16

HOW DO WE TREAT OUR IN-LAWS AND RELATIVES?

Some In-laws are good and some are not so good. Either way we cannot ignore their existence. They are our parents and they deserve the respect and honor. It is our turn as children to take care of our parents. Parents have a promise attached to them from God. The promise is so that we live long on this earth. The word of God says that children should honor their father and mother so that it will be well with them.

When a wife takes care of her own parents and ignores her husband's parents, then that is partiality. The husband might not address it but that does not mean he likes it. His actions begin to speak louder than words. He slowly detaches himself and eventually his heart hardens towards his wife. The way to a husband's heart is to love his parents and treats his relatives with love. Some in-laws are just difficult to love, but love them anyway. Eventually the light is going to shine.

Secret agendas or giving of things or money without the other knowing brings division and arguments in the home. The best way in dealing with In-laws is to exchange parents. For example, if the wife's parents want something, she should freely direct them to her husband. The same applies with the husband's parents; he should freely direct them to his wife. Wives it is our duty to make sure that we do not separate our husbands from their parents. We should unify.

The husband and wife should create a free atmosphere in their home and still stand firm on the rules of their home. We should be clear to let our parents know the rules of our home. There should not be a second guess as to who is who in the home by the way we treat each other before them. The In-laws position is to encourage, and love, not to dictate.

They should not show favoritism or cause division by hurtful words and actions. Unfortunately, some In-laws still want to run the show. In such cases, the husband as the head of the house has to establish the rules of his household.

Whoever comes has to abide within the rules. He has to stand firm on the principles of his home. He has to demonstrate that he is one with his wife and no man should separate them.

When the outside voice is louder than the inside voice then it brings chaos in the home. If there, is no one directing the traffic in the home, chaos and accidents are likely to happen. United we stand and divided we fall.

Exercise:

How is your relationship with your In-laws?

_____

_____

_____

_____

_____

How best can you improve the relationship?

_____

_____

_____

_____

_____

_____

_____

_____

_____

When is the next family reunion?

_____

_____

_____

_____

_____

_____

_____

_____

Discuss about those who cause problems and how you are going to deal with them.

_____

_____

_____

_____

_____

_____

_____

_____

Discuss how you are going to support the In-laws.

_____

_____

_____

_____

_____

_____

_____

_____

_____

_____

_____

_____

_____

_____

_____

_____

_____

Chapter 17

EDUCATION

Staying married takes knowledge. Knowledge is power therefore that we should invest in it. We acquire knowledge by learning. Learning is what we call education and it never ceases. Education in whatever area enhances you; it is a discipline and is healthy.

We do not stop learning the moment we do, we fall behind on many things. Education is not just getting degrees or bragging on how much we know, it is a discipline, which involves money and people skills as well.

Therefore, where money is involved what we do with it should not bring division in the home. Most homes break up because of money issues.

We have to be educated in the culture of whom we are marrying. When we say yes to each other in matrimony, we are also saying yes to the whole tribe. That means there is now an integration of both families. His family and her family become one. We then have to be prepared to face the good, the bad and the ugly on both sides of the families. There has to be wisdom, knowledge and understanding on how to handle such situations. There is nothing like well you take care of your own family (your parents and relatives) and I will take care of mine own parents and relatives. This type of mindset brings confusion and division in the home.

Most couples get married when they already have responsibilities. Responsibilities like taking care of siblings, paying tuition, and taking care of parents. Some parents need monitoring. Some are in nursing homes, and some need financial help. We should not ignore out parents especially in their old age. They took care of us so we should return the favor.

Attending marriage seminars helps a lot. It creates a good bonding and a better understanding on marriage.

It takes great communication skills in laying a good foundation on everything. Couples have to learn how to calculate their finances and see what is possible and build from there. Plan together and come to a solid agreement on how each need is going to be met education wise.

There has to be freedom of choice in choosing what to study. We do not impose on each other on what to study. We should give each other freedom of choice on what to study. If the husband has a PhD and the wife does not have any certificate in anything whatsoever, then the husband should encourage his wife to come up higher where he is. It is not how high you go; it is how many you are helping others get to where you are. We crown people according to how they make others better. Husband and wife should make each other better in every area of life. Love is the key.

Encourage each other to read books, finish the degree, take classes and increase in knowledge. Great minds read books. Find areas both of you need improvement and attend seminars. If you have never travelled plan a trip get out of your comfort zone and explore the world. Learn different cultures and that broadens your education.

Marriage is oneness, doing unto others; as you would want them do unto you. Therefore, the husband and wife should be happy for each other in making sure that each excels when it comes to education. Couples should grow together in every area of their life.

Sometimes listening to conversations among couples, you hear the husband referring to his wife as ignorant and know nothing or the wife saying the same about her husband, which is pride. Pride comes before a fall. The moment one feels they are better, puffed up, starts looking down on others, that is pride.

Pride does not stay on the throne. The husband and wife should compete on how to make each other better. The purpose of marriage is to be on the same team, with same goals and thriving in making each other better than they found each other.

Education in whatever area of life is a discipline, therefore husband and wife should help each other learn, attend seminars, be well versed in business and day today life. An idle mind is engages in unnecessary battles.

Exercise:

How important is education to you?

_____

_____

_____

_____

_____

_____

_____

What plans do you have for your education 5-10 years from now?

_____

_____

_____

_____

_____

_____

Do you have siblings or relatives you are paying tuition and how are you resolving that as a couple?

_____

_____

_____

_____

_____

_____

_____

_____

Do you have plans for paying your school loans?

_____

_____

_____

_____

_____

_____

_____

_____

Chapter 18

MARRIAGE ALWAYS WINS!

Marriage always wins when you keep at it. Every marriage has issues. Keep your eyes on the price it gets better with time. Marriage is a marathon not a hundred-meter dash. Strong Communication and the ability to execute is the key. If you do not give up marriage always wins. In order to have your happily ever after, there are rules, regulations and penalties that the players have to know in the game of marriage. The husband and wife have to understand that they are a team routing for the same goal.

The husband and wife have to know that their game is not against each other but for each other. There is constant communication between husband and wife in order for them to make a touchdown. Every day they practice and hustle, they are focusing on the trophy. They learn from their mistakes, then go back, and play again. They learn from their mistakes, then go back, and play again. They get bruised, wounded, win and sometimes lose but they do not take their eyes off the trophy. The trophy is to get old together and happily married.

The husband is the quarterback the visionary, and the wife is the wide receiver. Honor and respect makes the husband throw a good ball to the wife. When she catches the vision (ball) from her husband, she is well able to run with it and make a touchdown A touch down is when the husband and wife look at each other and say well done, we have loved each other to the end.

Regrouping and studying their enemy is what they do constantly. Words like I love you, I am here for you, I appreciate you, I am sorry, and above all thank you, always gives a good throw from the husband and an easy touchdown from the wife.

Penalties to name the few:

- resentment:
- criticism
- breaching of trust
- infidelity
- no touch or laughter
- drifting away from each other
- lying, spending too much money
- poverty, lack of leadership
- cheating
- bad friends,
- lack of prayer
- ridicule, abuse anger
- lack of respect and honor,

Remember the banner of winning the game in marriage is love, love each other until death do you part. When there is a mutual understanding and love being the anchor between the husband and wife marriage always wins! This is where couples have to get back to their basics, which is *love unspeakable.*

Notes

_____

_____

_____

_____

_____

_____

_____

_____

_____

_____

_____

_____

_____

_____

_____

_____

_____

_____

Chapter 19

LOVE UNSPEAKABLE

Always remember that the course meal for marriage is *love unspeakable*. One might ask, "what is love unspeakable and why mention it now?" This chapter is like saving the best for last. It is for you to fall back on when the storms of marriage come swinging back at you. It is more of a reminder, it takes you back to the time you set eyes on each other and eventually said I do. If your marriage is at a point of no return, and you have tried everything in your power to make things right, and still no sign of change, then I would urge you to revisit love unspeakable.

Have you ever seen a man and woman in love, they make time for each other. This kind of love between the man and the woman is what draws the two into marriage.

Do you remember the day you set your eyes on each other, and never wanted to let go? The feelings and the desires of wanting to be together, and not getting enough of each other is what we are going to revisit.

Love is very strong and it cuts deeper than any two edged sword. You hear couples say we will not have sex until we are married why because love unspeakable is respectful. It is a seal from God. This love will keep your marriage on the move. It is what caused you to wait for your honeymoon to be intimate.

Sometimes we have to remind each other of the days of our courtship to keep our relationships fresh. Couples should not short-circuit themselves when it comes to romance, or intimacy, why, because that is what glues the marriage together. We do not outgrow romance or intimacy infect it gets better the longer we are together. Love unspeakable has an aroma that draws the couples together. Its aroma is contagious and it is priceless.

There is no price tag to this love; it runs deeper than the ocean and the sky is no limit. You feel it and it is unexplainable. You talk on the phone for hours and never get tired. You look at each other's pictures and never get tired. The best way to quench this thirst is to be together. It makes a man and woman act as if they have lost their mind. When there is a good grip on this, then couples are able to stay together understanding why they married each other in the first place.

"When I looked at you through the eyes of a dove, with singleness of heart, I loved you and brought you to myself. When I brought you to myself, I married you."

These words of love overflow from a husband who has found his wife and is head over heels with the wife of his youth.

"There are threescore queens and fourscore concubines and virgins without number. My dove, my undefiled is but ONE; she is the only one of her mother; she is the choice one of her that bears her. The daughters saw her and blessed her yea the queens and the concubines, and they praised her". Songs of Solomon 6:8-9.

Couples can stay married for a long time loving each other when they go back to this first love.

When married couples have a good grip of this love, each time difficult times arise, they are able to resolve them with no malice. This love matures with us until we give it its proper place in marriage.

When you hear someone say, I found love, he/she is talking about love unspeakable. It is a secret package in everyone's heart. It is a life of romance and happily ever after. This love makes the husband leave his mother and father and cleave to his wife.

He is always on guard to stop any floods set to destroy the love. He protects and defends the love and his wife guards it to the end. Once it is lost, it takes time to get it back because it is so fragile.

Losing sight of this love makes marriage unbearable and miserable. When you hear people say, "Oh this couple has lost affection for each other," what they mean is that love unspeakable is no longer present.

I am not a marriage counselor, or a therapist, what I am relating to is through experience, observation and through the learning of the word of God. The violations of love unspeakable are adultery and fornication.

This love got us in trouble when we hit adolescence because we did not know how to harness it. Boys and girls try to understand the feelings they are having. They are not mature enough to understand, they are in the process of understanding.

Teenagers would be saying, "If my parents find out I would be in big trouble so I better not tell. If I tell them how I am feeling, I am going to be in trouble, I should not have boyfriend or girlfriend." There is war of right and wrong in the mind of an adolescent. The faucet of love unspeakable has started to flow and yet not to its maximum.

It gets to its maximum when people are married. Remember, love unspeakable is our seal from God. It matures when the man and woman say, I do. Instead of panicking and punishing every move, parents should embark on guiding, leading and mentoring their kids. Most kids have fallen off the creek because both parents neglected this stage.

Love Unspeakable, if not well harnessed can drives people crazy! It makes teenagers run away from home because they fail to harness it. As we mature enough we realize that this kind of love is different from the way we love our parents, teachers, brothers, or sisters.

It is love that is deeply rooted in a relationship with someone we want to spend our life together. When it is matures, It becomes reserved, it is not after intimacy meaning having sex before marriage but waits until marriage. It is respectful, and it is looks forward to marriage.

It forces you to be the person of your word, does not mix with shady stuff, stand by itself defends itself and it can take you places. It finds the one it loves; it feels like a gushing faucet running out of genuineness. It is a very good feeling that one has towards her/his soul mate when love unspeakable is in motion.

You hear couples say we are waiting for marriage; what they mean is they are going to give each other love unspeakable on their honeymoon, and from there it is going to be their fulfillment in their marriage.

Love unspeakable has a target, it is not just for anyone, it is like a search light, or an antenna, it is after the one to be with in matrimony.

It has a mind of its own, dances to its own tune, and has the eyes of a dove. There is no confusion, or fakeness about love unspeakable, what it does is that it leads you to fulfillment.

Waters cannot quench it; neither can floods drown it, it is like you run out of words to describe it. Once you experience it, you do not want anything less.

"Set me as a seal upon thine heart as a seal upon thine arm: for love is strong as death, jealousy is cruel as the grave: the coals thereof are coals of fire, which hath a most vehement flame. Many waters cannot quench love; neither an floods drown it if a man would give all the substance of his house for love it would utterly despise."

Songs of Solomon 8:6-7.

It is the kind of love married couples should give and willing to receive from each other. There has to be willingness to receive it. This love is for one wife one husband. You cannot double cross it.

A good example is that of Solomon. Solomon had love in him, but he misused his love, the bible says he loved women, and these women turned his heart to worship idols. He should have kept his love for the one wife he describes in the bible. This love gives couples the strength to overcome issues that come to separate them because it is an anchor, and a pillar of their love life in their marriage.

Love unspeakable cannot be adulterated or fornicated. When violated, it becomes toxic. The couples start to say, "But we used to love each other; we do not know what happened." What has happened here is that love unspeakable is no longer working for them but against them.

Reverse gear of love unspeakable.

When issues arise in the home and they are left unresolved for a long time, love unspeakable begins to dwindle. There is a tendency of losing interest in each other and gradually closing in. Double mindedness, is the blockage that refuses you to receive love or give love, it has a source.

Instead of your marriage looking like a rainbow, beautiful colors, it becomes so dull like the sun in the clouds. The question then is, "where is the blockage coming from what is the root cause, where did one open the door where did the love go?" When the door of uncertainty in marriage is wide open, your mind starts to wonder. Unfortunately, love unspeakable will always find a void and fills it.

This is a critical time because temptation will be knocking on your door. Therefore, whom do you want to give your love? If you do not give it to your wife/husband, you are definitely going to fill that void by giving it to someone else

Let us not lie to each other; there is a level of commitment required in love before we waste each other's time.

As the heart hardens towards each other then you start to hear infidelity, cheating, abuse, and unfaithfulness in the marriage. The love is now in reverse gear.

The problem with love unspeakable is that when not harnessed the right way it becomes toxic. When the love is violated it reverts, and it starts to attack itself, meaning what was good is now bad what was bad is now good but the end results is death no more life.

When there are blockages, in a relationship then the love unspeakable becomes a revolving door, someone is coming in, and someone is going out. What happens in a revolving door is that most people in there do not know each other. If one asks someone in the revolving door how it feels to be in there, most will not tell you much, because they are waiting to get out and go their way, a revolving door is not their destination; it is just a door for whoever is in it.

Love unspeakable in marriage is a permanent door with its hinges intact. When love unspeakable is no longer present, couples begin to act as if they are strangers. They start to act as if they do not know each other.

Most marriages start to become common; it begins to sound like a broken record that is playing over and over the same song, why, because the love has become rusty.

When someone smears mud on you, the best way to remove it is to let it dry and then remove it. Just remove the dry mud on your love and you can start to love again. Love unspeakable can be on hold when not appreciated.

People do not fall out of love or do not have love any more as per say, love is always there. It is either you have parked it somewhere, or you have put it on hold. Love will always find a void and fills it.

If you are honest with yourself, and search deep within yourself, you will discover that you have shifted your love to something else, only not for your spouse anymore. The good thing is you can still pick it up, and continue to love, yes; it is true you can pick it up, and keep on loving when you change your heart. We are making changes every day, changes for the good or for the bad.

We have to renew our minds when it comes to loving each other. The things, which are trying to divert your love, are temporary when you cultivate your love unspeakable.

This love should continue when we realize that it is not all the stuff we have, but who we have who is with us, and whose we are.

It should not grow old; it should be new every morning just like the mercies of the Lord. The mercies of the Lord are new every morning and great is his faithfulness.

You hear people say I can climb the highest mountain to come to you, or I can swim across the ocean just to get to you, all these expressions are telling how much head over heels one is in love. This love makes you feel like you can fly even if you do not have wings. It makes you feel like you can fly the airplane even if you are not a pilot; it is unexplainable, unspeakable and yet there.

I remember when my fiancé, now my husband, called me at work one morning from overseas. I had written down everything I wanted to say to him, but at that moment, I ran out of words. Ellen my friend was waving and pointing to the paper across my face. I could not even see anything, just his voice made me numb.

I was just smiling but no words were coming out of my mouth. When I look back at that scenario my love unspeakable was out of words. I just had this love in my heart for him I could not explain it.

The challenge comes on how to continue experiencing this love in our marriages. One might ask, "Is it still possible for couples to continue in that kind of love?" Yes, it is still possible because you are now looking at it on a different note. Two is better than one. It will not be practice time any more but playing the real game of marriage. As long as you keep your eyes on the price, all that will appear as giants in your marriage will be a done deal. Love is the key.

David when he went to the battlefield where his brothers were. Goliath had been fuming threats after threats to the children of Israel. When David heard the blasphemy, he looked at Goliath and said you are a done deal, and he looked at the people and asked what he was going to get when he killed Goliath. He did not focus on the problem but on the price. Do not waste your time on the fumes of issues in your marriage, regroup, and see each other with the eyes of love, the love that you had from the beginning.

We have not really experienced yet what God had in mind when he created Adam and Eve. He is just waiting for us to ask him and he is able to shows us how we should love each other in our marriages. He is the one with the blue print. He knows what nutrients we need in order to have a healthy marriage. There is nothing as sickening as eating, and yet you do not get full, they say empty calories do not fill you up, meaning you are eating refined foods, which do not have the nutrients any more. Our marriages should have the right nutrients so that we get full and be satisfied.

Love unspeakable is pricy

Yes, there is a price to pay in everything worthwhile keeping. Love unspeakable can cost you, even though the dividends are great. Sometimes people do not want to take time to do their homework. They do not read books on marriage. Couples have to be well versed in small things that affect the big things in marriage. We are in such a rush to get married, and we believe every word we tell each other with no evidence at all.

We sort of brain wash each other, then in the long run we find half of what we said to each other was not true. We need to go beyond what we tell each other find out more information. Take your prerequisites before you engage in marriage.

Marriage is into the details. I am saying this to say that one should not get into marriage blindly. Marriage is a long-term not a short term, you swim upstream not downstream. Love unspeakable takes off when the runway is free.

Those who play football, soccer, or any game, they face so many obstacles. Some of the players sprain their legs, some have concussions, some hurt their knees, but they all have one focus, go to the finals, win the game, and bring the trophy home.

A good marriage is a process; this process is patience, un-forgiveness, friendship and unconditional love. God wants us to experience love unspeakable all the time. Unfortunately, when we go through many rough times in our marriages we tend to put so much emphasis on the problems than the solutions. When couples start to harden their hearts against each other, love unspeakable is at risk.

Our marriages are as a diamond covered in dross. It goes through the fire, through water, and through the beating. All we are mesmerized with is the finished product, not the process. Marriage is a process with well paying dividends. Those who are able to overcome all kinds of storms; they are the ones who will enjoy the benefits of love unspeakable. We cannot afford to put our love unspeakable at risk because it is our navigator, our GPS and our compass. It has to navigate in the skies as us and fly this airplane of marriage. Love unspeakable yields to the main coach who is God. His rules, just to mention a few are commitment, covenant, counseling, love, honest, and faithfulness.

If there is, something I would want to stress on more is that we do not lose our love; issues come to distract us from loving each other. Issues in life can make us negative and bitter. They come to test our love unspeakable. We need to know that storms do not come to stay. Eventually the sun is going to shine. There is something unique about being married, it is a covenant and God honors a covenant. He becomes our partner as we engage in our marriages we are on the right track. In conclusion, no matter how difficult the situations may be, always bounce back to your *love unspeakable.*

Notes

_____

_____

_____

_____

_____

_____

_____

_____

_____

_____

_____

_____

_____

_____

_____

_____

_____

_____

_____

_____

_____

ABOUT THE AUTHOR

My name is Shelly Rudo Chapinduka. I am a mother of four with two grandsons and one on the way. My husband and I are ministers of the Gospel and we have been married for almost 37 years now. I am still looking forward to having many more years of fun, cuddling, laughter and loving each other. We came to America in 1987 with our two little children. The other two were born in Tulsa Oklahoma where my husband attended Oral Roberts University.

We then moved to Dallas Texas where we have been residing up to now. I want to thank all the families here in America, different ethnicities, which embraced us and made our stay here to be very comfortable. Thank you very much.

I was born in Zimbabwe Africa. My parents are late now but they are always present in my heart and in my mind. I grew up in the city and in the village. I learnt how to farm in a very young age and I still have the passion for farming.

I have one stepbrother and one late stepsister from my mum's side. On my father's side, I have four stepbrothers. My two stepbrothers have their own mum and my other two stepbrothers and I have our own separate mothers as well. Our father and our mothers are late except for one. I am glad that I found my stepbrothers and we love each other very much.

From a young age I always envisioned myself married and with kids. I promised myself in the third grade that I was going to pattern my marriage after my grandmother who worked on a farm. Her name was Marita and her husband's name was Phiri. They did not have much, lived in a one-room hut but they loved each other so much. They would laugh and smile at each other most of the time and it was such a joy to witness their relationship. I so wished my mum and dad had such a relationship. I did not grow up in a family where mum and dad loved each other. My dad was a police officer and because of his job, we moved from place to place.

Dad would treat me good but would fight constantly with mum. I remember the days I would cry myself to sleep.

I feared for the safety of my mum because my dad had a gun. When dad would come home drunk, I would be on the edge because I would not know how that evening would end up. It would take me time to go to sleep because most of the nights he would end up fighting with mum. Each time they fought, I would rush and separate them from the fight.

I was young, I always felt helpless, and hopeless each time my dad was beating on my mum. I have scars on my body of trying to separate my parents from fights. It still gives me chills when I think of it; no child should ever experience that type of life style. I grew up quickly and I felt like I had assumed a parental role to my parents. I felt like I missed a lot of my childhood and I never liked the feeling.

A home should be a place of rest not turmoil. These experiences made me angry and bitter but I could not show it. Occasionally when someone ruffled my feathers, I would feel the rage in me wanting to fight but would restrain myself. I did not know how to deal with the pain that I had internalized from my childhood. My dad loved me but he did not love my mum.

One time I asked my mum why she was still with my dad and she said it was because of me. She did not want to leave me alone with dad so that is why she stayed.

Domestic violence is terrible! It reduces a person to untold fear. Growing up I had promised myself that I was never ever going to have a marriage like my parents. To my surprise, my husband and I began to argue just like them. My husband's parents divorced when he was around five years old. His father was a police officer as well and his upbringing was even worse than mine was.

Different stepmothers took care of him, his brothers and his sister. His childhood was a disaster. He also had hidden anger issues and occasionally he would just burst out from nowhere. Our marriage was a volcano ready to erupt. We were two individuals with unresolved anger issues.

This is happening in most families. I am not here to expose my family. My desire is that we understand that most marriages have issues brooded from childhood. I leant how to pretend like everything was okay and yet I was wasting inside. I wondered why I was experiencing the same marital problems that I had promised myself never ever to have. My issues were more of outside voices finding their way into my marriage. Outside voice was much louder than the inside voice from the beginning of our marriage. Not everyone celebrates your marriage. Never allow the outside voice and the religious voices to be louder than the inside voice. The husband and wife are responsible for the turn out of their marriage. This is what religion does it makes you fear man (a generic term) more than God. Church should be like a hospital not a prison. It pricks God's heart to see his children whom he will have saved from the world come to church and be in bondage. A church is a healing place.

We were in the ministry and I had no one I could really tell my problems. Marital problems are even among the clergy, so please pray for those who minister the gospel all over the whole world. They are human beings with the same issues and still have to feed the flock. When you are in the ministry people look to you and they do not believe that you could also be having marital problems in your home.

I thank God that he never gave up on us it is by his grace that we are still together. We have come a long way and I believe we are in a position to help those struggling with the same issues as well. Remember divided we fall but united we stand. If I were to choose again, I would choose my husband

Paul. He is the one God confirmed to me and we loved each other and still love each other. If you want to experience the God kind of marriage, be truthful to self. When you understand that, you become your own critic and you learn to be faithful in public and in private. Marry the man/woman who loves you from his/her heart not for looks. Above all my friends, I would do you a disservice if I do not introduce you to my mentors who have been helping me in my marriage. They are the best coaches and are well able to help you walk this marital life.

They do not impose themselves on you; your freewill allows you to invite them. My mentors are God the father Jesus our Lord and Savior and the Holy Ghost. They are just a call away. You do not need a phone, all you do is open your mouth and talk to them.

All you say is, "Jesus I invite you to come into my heart, forgive me my sins and make me your child today."

It is so simple, life changing and eternal. Find yourself a good church and continue to grow in the Lord.

God bless you all!

www.ingramcontent.com/pod-product-compliance
Lightning Source LLC
Chambersburg PA
CBHW072244270326
41930CB00010B/2268